Prophecy
Written
in the Stars

or Did It Hurt
When You Fell From Heaven?

DR. LARRY ANDERSON, DBS
Glory Day and In the Spirit of Elijah Ministries

outskirts
press

Prophecy Written in the Stars
or Did It Hurt When You Fell From Heaven?
All Rights Reserved.
Copyright © 2021 Dr. Larry Anderson, DBS
v2.0

The opinions expressed in this manuscript are solely the opinions of the author and do not represent the opinions or thoughts of the publisher. The author has represented and warranted full ownership and/or legal right to publish all the materials in this book.

This book may not be reproduced, transmitted, or stored in whole or in part by any means, including graphic, electronic, or mechanical without the express written consent of the publisher except in the case of brief quotations embodied in critical articles and reviews.

Outskirts Press, Inc.
http://www.outskirtspress.com

ISBN: 978-1-9772-3197-0

Library of Congress Control Number: 2020917697

Cover Photo © 2021 Dr. Larry Anderson, DBS. All rights reserved - used with permission.

Outskirts Press and the "OP" logo are trademarks belonging to Outskirts Press, Inc.

PRINTED IN THE UNITED STATES OF AMERICA

Table of Contents

Introduction	i
Chapter One: God's Number Twelve	1
Chapter Two: Aquarius	6
Chapter Three: Virgo	12
Chapter Four: Scorpio	24
Chapter Five: Capricorn	32
Chapter Six: Aries	39
Chapter Seven: Cancer	48
Chapter Eight: Pisces	57
Chapter Nine: Gemini	63
Chapter Ten: Sagittarius	69
Chapter Eleven: Taurus	75
Chapter Twelve: Leo	85
Chapter Thirteen: Libra	91
Chapter Fourteen: Predestination or Did it Hurt when You Fell from Heaven?	99
Conclusion and Acknowledgments	101

Revelation 4:6
The four beasts around Gods' Throne

"And before the throne there was a sea of glass like crystal and in the midst of the throne and around about the throne were four beasts, and the first beast was like a Lion, and the second beast was like a Calf, and the third beast hid a Face of a Man, and the fourth beast was like a Flying Eagle."

These four beasts represent the Attributes of God.

The Lion represents Gods' Majestic Beauty and Power.

The Calf represents Gods' Faithfulness

The Man represents Gods' Intellectual Abilities

The Eagle represents Gods' Sovereignty

Introduction

This is the third book that I have written. In my first book, I wrote about my prophecy and what Jesus showed me in a dream. My second book was written for the benefit of those who have been called to the ministry of Jesus Christ and Gods word as church leaders. I am one of Gods "end time" minor prophets, there are others, I am sure of that. In my first book, I called myself an Acts 2:17, last days prophet. I must correct that. I am not a "last days" prophet. I misinterpreted that. Last Days would be an indication that it would be during a period we call the Tribulation. The Tribulation happens after Jesus comes back for His church. I don't want to be left here....LOL. I prefer to be "caught up" when Jesus returns Amen! So, it's end times prophet for me. Amen

This book is for everyone, it's different. There hasn't been a book written like this one in over 125 years. I told my sister that I am writing this book to show people why there is a D and an R in front of my name LOL.

God wrote the gospel stories in the stars, long before man could write and read.

It's recorded in the bible. I will take you on a ride through the astrological zodiac, and discover Gods Prophecies written in the Stars. Be amassed.

There are Twelve Astrological Constellations. Each Major Astrological Constellation has three more constellations that add to their Prophetic Meaning. I will guide you through their names and prophetic meanings.

Satan changed their meanings when he the father of deception, invented Horoscopes, and Divination.

Look what the Prophet Isaiah had to say about Satan's Astrology and Divination.

Isaiah 48:13

"Thou art wearied in the multitudes of counsels, let now the astrologers, star gazers, the monthly prognosticators, stand up and save yourself from these things that shall come on to thee."

Wow!!! You that practice these things are in deep trouble. Stand up and save yourselves.

When I was a young boy I loved to lay out in my front yard at night and stare up at the stars and constellations. My favorite constellation was Orion. I was told by someone that Orion represented a mighty warrior, I liked that.

Throughout my life I have had many coincidences, like when I served in the Navy. I was in a P-3 Orion Air squadron. Then, when I was studying in seminar, I discovered that the constellation Orion is a reprehensive type of Jesus coming back as "The Conquering Lion of Judah."

In the 1960s' the Hippies declared that it was "The Dawning of the Age of Aquarius." What a lie, Biblically, it was the end of the Age of Capricorn, and the Dawning of the Age of Aries. Biblically according to the prophecies written in the stars Aries is the "Born-Again Age." This age started when Luther broke from the Roman Catholic church, and printed the Bible, and men could read, and interpret Gods word. The bible gets its' name, Bible, from the town it was printed in. Praise the Lord for Luther Amen.

John 3:7

Nicodemus asked Jesus how he could get to heaven and Jesus replied.

"You must be Born-again."

All the Christian faiths pretty much confess to being Born-Again. If they don't they are a false Christian religion. I first heard about being born-again from the Pentecostals in 1972. By the Year 2000, most Christian faiths, had put this in the mission statements as a requirement to get to Heaven. Some are just learning about being born again, like the Lutherans. Read your churches mission statement. If you can not find them saying you must be born-again, then get out, they are false.

We will be looking at 48 constellations and their prophecies, and many stars with Hebrew meanings related to them. May this book be a Blessing to you that read it, in Jesus name Amen.

Dr. Larry Anderson, end of days prophet of God

CHAPTER ONE

God's Number Twelve

God is a God of numbers. I chose to start this book with God's number Twelve. Twelve broken down to its lowest denominator is three, the number of the Trinity.

Genesis chapter 49 tells us about the Twelve Tribes of Israel

There were Twelve Apostles. There are Twelve Signs of the Astrological Zodiac, and there are Twelve Months in a year, and Twelve Hours on our clocks.

Jacob's sons make up the Twelve Tribes of Israel. Let's take a look at them first.

Jacob assigned each of his brothers a tribe and an astrological sign as their standard.

Judah was assigned the constellation Leo.

Rueben was assigned the constellation Aquarius.

Zebulon was assigned the constellation Virgo.

Naphtali was assigned the constellation Capricorn.

Gad was assigned the constellation Aries.

Issachar was assigned the constellation Cancer.

Simeon was assigned the constellation Pisces.

Dan was assigned the constellation Scorpio.

Benjamin was assigned the constellation Gemini.

Asher was assigned the constellation Sagittarius.

Levi was assigned the constellation Libra.

Ephrain and Manasseh were assigned the constellation Taurus. These standards were posted in front of their camps. Each sign has a prophetic message. That is what we will be looking at in this book. Just what does each constellation really mean.

Some of the tribes had some notable people in them.

Judah had Jesus.

Dan had Samson.

Ephrain and Manasseh had the prophets Samuel, Gideon, Deborah, and Joshua.

Levi had four prophets, Moses and his brother Aaron, John the Baptist and Eli.

Naphtali had the prophet Elijah.

Benjamin had the Apostle Paul, Queen Ester, and King Saul, the first King of the Jewish people.

Psalm 147:4

"He tells us the number of stars, and He calls them by name."

The story of Jesus birth, death and resurrection, and return, is told in the stars.

The stars tell the Gospel Story through their prophetic messages. They tell of Jesus birth and death and resurrection. They tell us how He will come and Redeem us and destroy Satan. The whole story is there in the heavens.

Isaiah 40:26 "Lift up your eyes on high, and behold who has created these things that brings out the brightness. He calls them by their names, by the greatness of His might."

There were Twelve Apostles. Paul was the last Apostle; he was the Apostle to the Gentiles (us). Paul died in a Roman prison. John the youngest of the Apostles, he was sixteen when Jesus called him, John was sentenced to life in prison on the Island of Patmos, where he wrote the Book of Revelation, and then died at around the age of 80.

I was in a Sunday service at a Baptist church one Sunday morning, just day dreaming away the sermon when I heard the man that Jesus had sent to speak to me that day, say that the Apostle Peter, the oldest of the Apostles' was crucified upside down. That caught my attention and I was hooked. I just had to learn more about all this stuff, so I went to seminary to learn. I was on my way home, to Jesus Amen, the "Prodigal Son."

It's believed that the other nine apostles followed Peters lead and asked to be crucified upside down. When the Romans asked Peter why he wanted to be crucified upside down, his answer was "because I am nor worthy to be crucified the same as the Lord." Wow I like that.

God's Number Twelve

The Apostle

Peter

CHAPTER TWO

Aquarius

The Water Bear

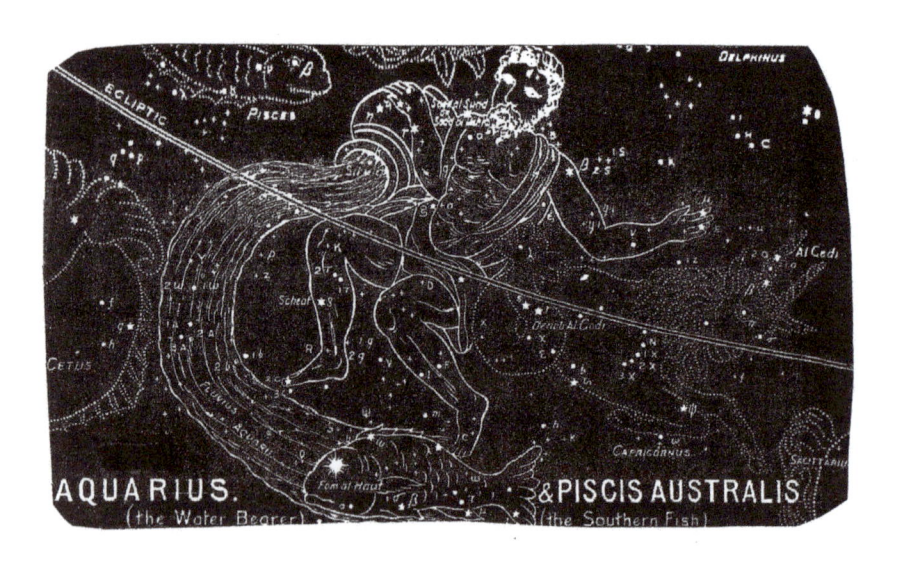

The River of Life

Chapter Two
Aquarius
The Water Bear
The Living Waters of Life

I am starting with the constellation Aquarius because it is one of the most important prophecies in the Bible and the Stars. The constellation Aquarius is a very good example of how Satan, the thief and liar has tried to deceive people with his satanic astrological zodiac. Satan says the sign Aquarius represents air; he calls it an Air Sign. Satan takes the four signs of nature and divides them into threes. Three water signs constellations; Cancer, Pisces, and Scorpio, three fire signs constellations; Aries, Leo, and Sagittarius, three earth signs constellations; and three air signs constellations. The conflict here is that Aquarius is called a Water Bearer, and God doesn't separate the zodiac into four categories. Aquarius in Gods' Zodiac represents "The Holy Spirit" pouring out the River of Life, it delivers the living waters of life. Jesus said, "drink of this water, and Never thirst again." Amen

The Holy Spirit has many natures. The first was to impregnate Mary with Jesus. The second is to be sent to us as our Comforter.

John 14:15-16 "If you love me, keep my commandments, and I will pray to my father, and He will send you another comforter (Holy Spirit). It will abide with you forever, even the Spirit of Truth."

When we accept Jesus as the Lord of Lords, He prays to God the Father for us, asking Him to send us a comforter. Jesus is the intercessor for us, our redeemer, He is the one who prays for us to receive the comforter. The Holy Spirit is the one who delivers our prayers to Jesus. The Holy Spirit is our prayer interrupter.

The Holy Spirit is the one who watered the "dry bones" of Israel.

This started in 1918 when the Jewish people started to return to their country then called Palestine, this was after the Ottoman wars, and was complete May 15, 1948, when Israel once again was recognized as a Nation.

Isaiah 32: 1-2 "as a river of water in a dry place.

Isaiah 51:6 "making her a wilderness like Eden, and her deserts like a garden of the Lord."

Numbers 24:7 "He will pour the water out of His buckets.'

Ezekiel 36:24-28 "sprinkled clean and given a new heart." Amen

Israel has been Born-Again.

The Holy Spirits last act will be during the Great Tribulation.

Acts 2:17 "In the last days, I shall pour my spirit out on All flesh."

This is when those didn't believe before the "catching up" suddenly realize: that Jesus did come, and they start to profess that Jesus is the Lord and the Anti- Christ martyrs them. They are the ones in Revelation, that are in White Robes before the Throne of God, asking Him when will they be revenged?

This constellation has 108 stars. A Hebrew name of one star gives us a meaning is *Melik* "a record of pouring forth.' Another star named *Deli* means "the Water Urn."

There are three supporting constellations to Aquarius prophecy, they are; Pisces Australis, Pegasus, and Cygnus.

Aquarius

In the picture you can see the water being poured out of the Urn and onto the head of the Fish Pisces Australis, the Southern Fish which is half of the constellation Pisces.

Pisces Australis
The Northern Fish

This constellation prophecy represents the Redemptive work of Jesus. The: northern fish of Pisces is reprehensive of the vessel that is taking the dead in Christ to a safe haven in heaven. It is pointing towards heaven.

This constellation has 22 stars.

Chapter Two
Pegasus
The Lead Horse

The Hebrew words Pega meaning "Chief" and Sus meaning "Horse"

Pegasus
The Winged Horse

To understand this constellation prophecy, we have to look at the Hebrew words associated with some of the stars in it. The word *Pega* means "Chief" and the word *Sus* means "Lead Horse." The Hebrew word *Markab* adds to the meaning of the prophecy with this "returning from afar." The Hebrew word *Scheat* means "who goes and returns." To understand this, we need to understand one of The Holy Spirits commissions. The Holy Spirit delivers our prayers to Jesus daily. It is coming and going constantly. The Holy Spirit is a Blessing from Jesus Amen, and connects us to God the Father.

Cygnus
The Swan

This constellations prophecy is again, the coming quickly of the Holy Spirit. It is a picture of a Huge Bird in Flight. Its' wings are large and spread wide. It is facing the Heavens. It has webbed feet, having come from the river of life. This is the Holy Spirit at work. What a wonderful blessing Amen.

CHAPTER THREE

Virgo
The Hope of Israel

Virgo
The Hope of Israel

Chapter Three
Virgo
The Virgin Hope of Israel

Virgo represents the prophecy that God would select Mary, to be "The Hope of Israel." And that she would conceive the "promised seed of Israel," Jesus, "the hope of all nations." This constellation was assigned to the Tribe of Zebulon. It has 110 stars.

Genesis 3:15 is important to the prophecy of this constellation.

"I will put enmity between you and the women. And you shall bruise His heal, and He shall rise, and He shall bruise your head."

Mary was the hope to conceive the hope of all nations.

The prophecy is that God blessed women with children, who are our hope Amen! And that He put them between women and the devil.

This prophecy is being fulfilled every day.

The Hebrew named star I found in this constellation is Bethulah, which means "Virgin."

Isaiah 7: 14 and again in Matthew 1: 23 we find this:

"Behold a virgin shall conceive and bear a son, and shall call Him Immanuel."

Aratus sang this song, "Beneath Boötes feet, the virgin seek."

Isaiah 9: 6-7 says this:

"for unto us a child is born, unto us a son is given, and the government shall be on His shoulders."

The three constellations associated with prophecy are Coma, Centaurus, Virgos and Boötes.

Keep Your Eyes on the Master

Coma
The Arrival of the Desired One

Located right next to Virgo

Coma
The Arrival of the Desired One

This constellation is located next to Virgo, and it is a picture of a women holding a child. This is the prophecy that Mary would deliver Jesus, "The promised seed." The hope of all Nations.

Haggai 2: 7 "The desire of All Nations."

This prophecy has been fulfilled. This constellation has 43 stars in it. It is believed the "The Star of Bethlehem," that lead the Wise Men to Jesus, appeared in this constellation at Jesus birth.

Numbers 24: 7

"There shall come a star out of Jacob, and a scepter shall rise out of Israel. Matthew 24: 7

"And there shall appear a sign of "The Son of Man," in the heavens."

Shakespeare wrote this about Coma, in his "Titus Andronicus," "Good boy in Virgo's lap."

The Son has two natures, "the son of man" and "the son of God."

The first nature has been fulfilled. Jesus suffered as a man here on earth.

Centaurus
The Centaur

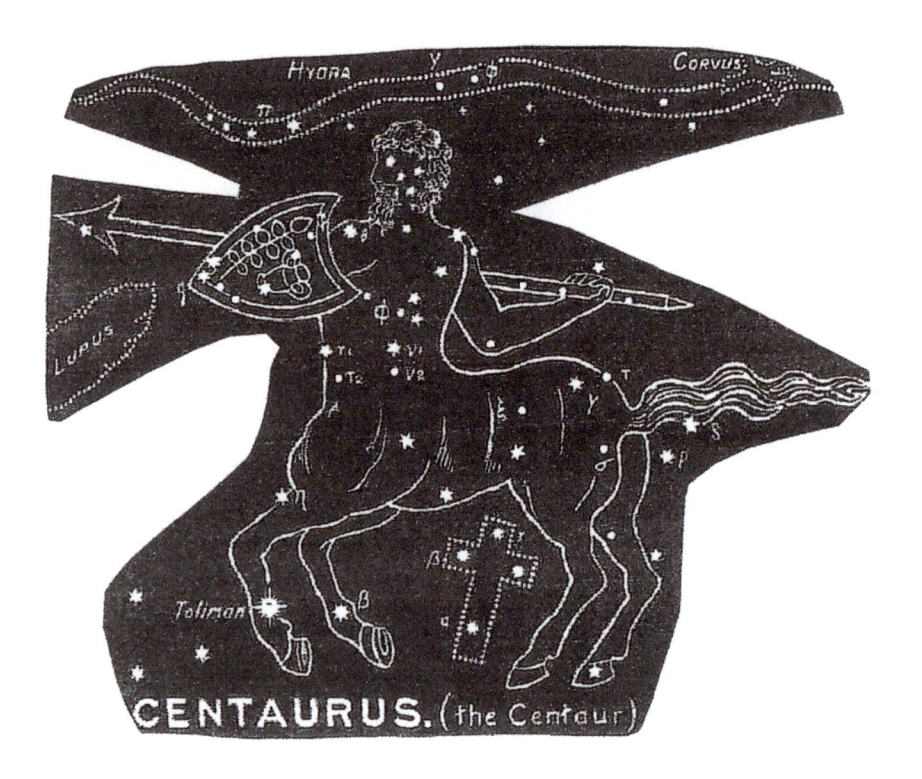

Centaurus
The Centaur

This constellations prophecy is that after being despised and abused, Jesus will return, as a Mighty Warrior, like non have ever seen. Half man and half horse swiftly moving forward, with a shield (the Holy Spirit) and a mighty spear (God). He is coming for Satan and all his demons.

This prophecy is yet to be fulfilled. Wow unto all of God's enemies.

It's not to late, but I wouldn't be one to hesitate. I wouldn't want to face Him without His Mercy and His Grace, on the Judgment Day.

Revelation 1: 8 "I am the Alpha and the Omega, the beginning and the end."

Luke 2: 40 "and that as a man having two natures."

Isaiah 53: 3 "He is despised and rejected by men. A man of sorrows and grief." He was despised and we esteem Him not."

This constellation has 35 stars. *Bezeis* is a Hebrew word for "despised."

 Below the constellation Centaurus lays the Southern Cross, indicating the "Final Judgment," been made. The Redeemer is coming.

Boötes
The Coming One
He who comes

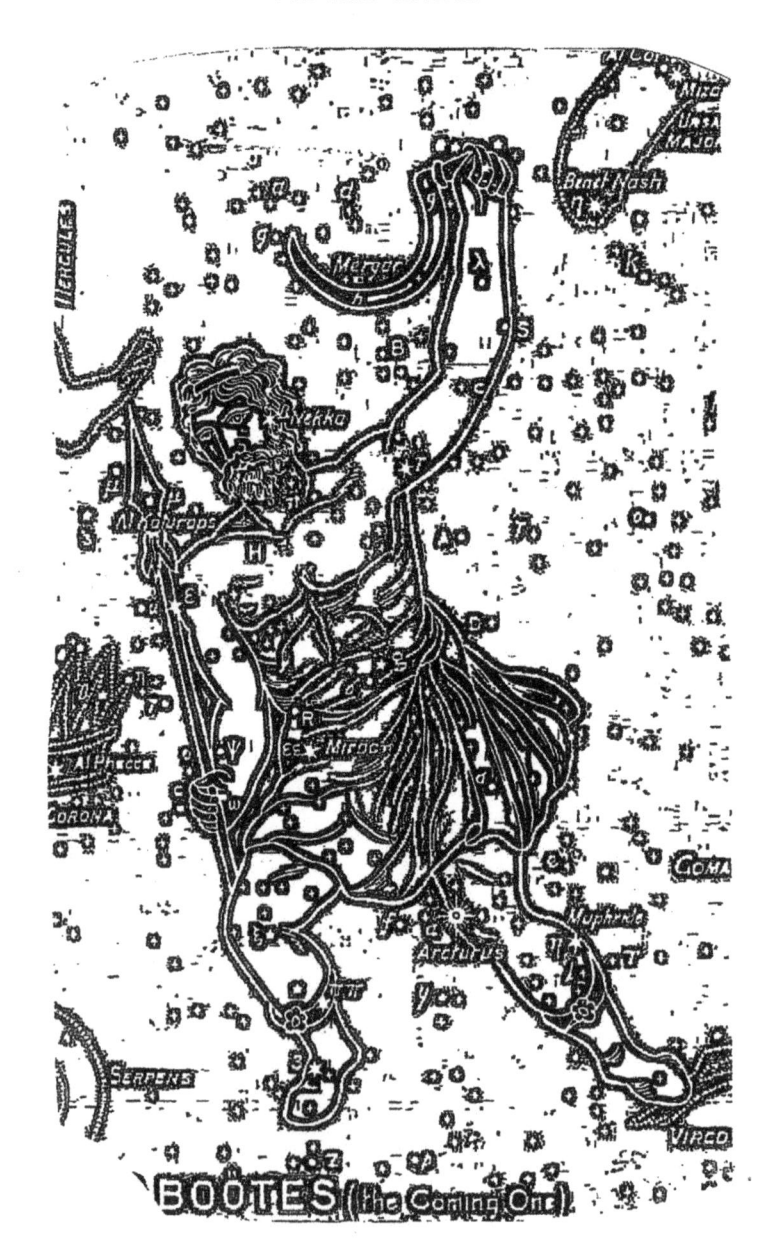

Revelation 6:7
Death

"And when he opened the fourth seal, I heard a voice of the fourth beast say, come see and I looked, and behold a *Pale Horse*, and his name that sat on him was Death, and Hell followed with him."

Boötes
The Coming One
He Who Comes
The Angel of Death

This is an interesting constellation. Boötes represents Jesus as "the Angel of Death." He is coming to piecing and bruising, Judge. In His right hand is a Large Spear (God), and in His left hand is a Sickle (the Holy Spirit).

The Hebrew word *Bo*, means "to come."

Psalm 95: 13

"for He comes, for Judgment of the earth; He shall judge the world in Righteousness, and the people with His truth."

Another Hebrew word *Merga*, means "one who bruises."

This prophecy will be fulfilled at "The Battle of Armageddon."

The Great Harvester comes for the ungodly, the unbelievers, those who are blind to the gospels and God's word.

Revelation 14; 15-16

"I looked; and behold, a white cloud, and upon the cloud one sat like "the son of man." And another Angel came out with a loud voice to Him that sat on the cloud, thrust your sickle and reap."

The Angel of Death, the Grim Reaper.

This prophecy will be fulfilled very soon.

Virgo

So, look up, and be watchful

For the end is near

It is written in the stars and our gospels

Our home is not here

So, look up and be watchful

And don't be left behind.

Look Up

CHAPTER FOUR

Scorpio

The Scorpion, attack of the enemy, the seducer

Crushed by the foot of the Redeemer

Chapter Four
Scorpio
The Scorpion
Attack of the enemy
The seducer

Scorpio
The Scorpion, attack of the enemy, the seducer

This is an interesting constellation its' prophecy is this; the Life, Death and Rebirth of Jesus. Its prophecies show how Scorpio the enemy, attacked Jesus, bruising His heal in death, and how Jesus rose from the dead (rebirth), this part of Scorpios prophecy has been fulfilled. Scorpio has three constellations that support this prophecy. They are Serpens the serpent, Ophiuchus the serpent holder, and Hercules the mighty vanquisher. This constellation was assigned to the Tribe of Dan. It has 44 stars. There are two stars with Hebrew names, Akrab, meaning "war and conflict" and *Lesath*, meaning "perverse.

Jesus had many conflicts, like in the wilderness with Satan, and in the garden of Gethsemane, where He sweat blood, and on the cross, where He died. His earthly conflicts are over for now. He comes back as a Mighty Conquer.

Exodus 1 tells us the Satan wants to destroy the seed of Abraham.

2 Kings 11 says; 'the kings Son is rescued."

Matthew 2, writes about Jesus genealogy saying this, Herod the King put out an order to slay all the baby boys born the year, Jesus was born.

Revelation 9: 3-6

"And their torment was as a Scorpion's sting, sent by God to all His enemies. And there came out smoke, locusts upon the earth, and unto them was given power, as the Scorpions of the earth have power.

Psalm 9: 3

"thou shalt tread upon the lion, and the adder, and the young lion, and the dragon, shalt thou trample under feet."

In the picture Hercules (Jesus) steps on the scorpion's heart, crushing it, and you can see Lupus (Satan's demon angels) also falling in death. This prophecy is yet to be fulfilled. It will be fulfilled at the Battle of Armageddon.

Satan the father of lies, the thief and seducer, will pay the cost for stealing Jesus crown.

Serpens
(The serpent)
Ophiuchus
(The Serpent Holder)

God and the Devil

Scorpio

Hercules
(The Mighty One)

The Mighty Vanquisher

Serpens, Ophiuchus, and Hercules

Serpens, *the Serpent*

This constellations prophecy is that the great old serpent Satan will be caught and held for a time. This will happen after the Battle of Armageddon. When God throws Satan that old serpent, bound in chains, into the bottomless pit, for 1,000 years. The Hebrew stars in this constellation names are; *Unuk*, meaning "encompassing," and *Alyah*, meaning "the accursed." There are 134 stars in Serpens. A long slithering snake.

Satan the thief, has stolen the crown, but he will lose it to the Risen Christ. This prophecy is yet to be fulfilled.

Ophiuchus, *the Serpent Holder*

This constellations prophecy is that God will come and grab the serpent and hold him until the judgment day (Great White Throne Judgment). Ophiuchus is pictured hold the serpent with both hands, while stepping on the scorpions heart and crushing Satan's demons (the scorpion). Above Him is his companion, Hercules with a large club. To the right are Libra's scales, ready to make the final judgment and balance the sin debt, as paid in full. There are two Hebrew names of stars they are: *Afeichus*, meaning "the serpent held," and *Triophas*, meaning, "treading under foot." This prophecy is yet to be fulfilled.

Hercules *The Mighty Vanquisher*

This constellations prophecy is that Jesus (Hercules) is victorious at the battle of Armageddon.

In the picture you see in His left hand is a three headed monster (Satan's demon angles). He has a large club in His right hand, getting ready to strike the three headed monster. On His head is the lions head, and He is girded with a bow and arrows. Satan's crown is falling upside down, and birds of prey are swiftly approaching to eat the monster. Lyra the burning altar, is near.

David prophesied this 4,000 years ago.

Psalm 91; 13 "thou shall tread upon the lion and adder, the young lion and the dragon shall you trample under foot.'

It's time for a miracle, it's time for restoration, it's time for revival.

CHAPTER FIVE

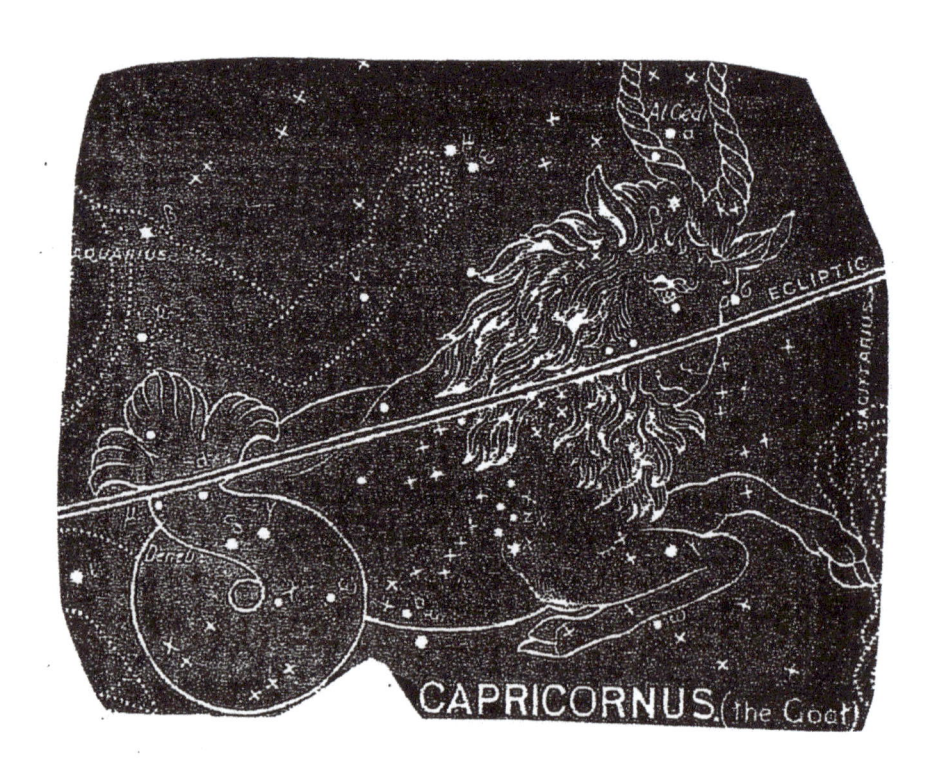

Capricorn
The Goat

Capricorn
The Goat

In ancient Israel (Canaan Land) the goat would represent a "sacrificial animal." Jesus was the sacrificial Lamb of God.

In this prophecy we see the goat being ate by the fish. This represents the death and rebirth of Jesus (Born-Again). It is a type of the "catching up' of the church. In a winkling of an eye, we will be changed.

This constellation was assigned to the Tribe of Naphtali and has 51 stars. The Hebrew word *Deneb al Gedi*, means "the sacrifice comes." Another Hebrew word *Al Gedi*, means "kid or goat."

There are three constellations associated with its prophecy they are Sagitta, Aquila, and Delphinus.

Part of this prophecy has been fulfilled. Jesus was sacrificed and has risen from the dead. The next part of the prophecy involves the dead in Christ, who will rise first, then a mystery is revealed, "some of us will go to heaven alive."

I Thessalonians chapter four and I Corinthians chapter 15, Paul reveals a mystery of the Old testament.

This is my prophecy from my other books, "Jesus is coming in my life time"....Amen....I am going to heaven alive.

Remember my friends "It is always darkest, just before dawn....cornova virus amen.

Sagitta (The Arrow)
Aquila (The Eagle)
Delphinus (The Dolphin)

The Redeemed

Sagitta
The Arrow of God

This constellation might surprise some of you. It is "the arrow of God," that pieces Jesus, killing Him.

Job 6:4

"the arrows of the almighty are with in me."

Psalms 38: 2

"thine arrows stick fast to me, and thy hand pressed me sore.'

Isaiah 53; 4-5

"He was wounded for our transgressions."

   The Hebrew word *Sham,* means "destroying."

This constellation has 18 stars, it is small, its prophecy has been fulfilled.

Aquila
The Eagle, the smitten one falling

In this constellation we find the prophecy that Jesus has been smitten, we see the eagle falling out of the sky. It represents the dying savior. This constellation has 74 stars.

Psalm 38: 2 "my heart Paneth, my strength fails me, as for the light of mine eyes, it is gone from me," the arrows sticks to me fast."

Zechariah 13: 6 "and one shall say to him, "what are these wounds in you hands?" Then he shall answer, "those with I was wounded in the house of friends."

Father forgive them for they know not what they do.

Delphinus
The Dead One Rising

This constellation completes the born-again phase. It has been happening since Jesus was crucified. It is an ongoing process with the people here on earth. Jesus was the first to rise from the dead and be born-again, the Saints will be next. This constellation has 18 stars. The picture shows the new born fish, after eating the goat.

Capricorn

A Mystery is Solved
1 Thessalonians Chapter 4 verses 16-18

Prophecy Written in the Stars

Gabriel Blows on His Horn

The Dead in Christ Raise First

CHAPTER SIX

Aries
The Ram

Chapter Six
Aries
The Ram

This is an interesting constellation whos' prophecy fits the Biblical Age that we are now in. This is a picture of the Born-Again Lamb (Jesus). After coming out of the dark ages, we were given the written gospels, and told Jesus is our redeemer. Those in the Old Testament had no redeemer. Before that all they had were the stars to tell the gospel story. When Jesus arrived, The Holy Bible was written, but not put in its' present order. The biblical age of Aries started in the 1400's, when the written word was finally put in order. This is when this prophecy was fulfilled. The lamb of God had risen in Spirit, and was now available to us. Praise the Lord Amen.

El Natik is a Hebrew word meaning "wounded or slain."

Al Sheratan means "bruised or wounded."

John 3:5-7 "Verily (The truth) verily, I say unto you, Except a man be born water and of the Spirit, he cannot enter into the kingdom of God.

John 1:29 "Behold the Lamb of God which takes away the sin of the world."

Revelation 5:12 "Worthy is the Lamb, without blemish, without spot."

The goat in the previous chapter was sacrificed on the cross, and reborn the Lamb of God, in Aries.

Jesus was Baptized as a man in water, born-again in the spirit, and rose from the dead, a new unblemished Lamb of God.

This sign was assigned to the Tribe of GAD. It has 66 stars. The three supporting constellations are, Cassiopeia, Cetus, and Perseus.

Cassiopeia
(The Enthroned Woman)
The Captive Delivered, and Preparing for Her Husband, the Redeemer

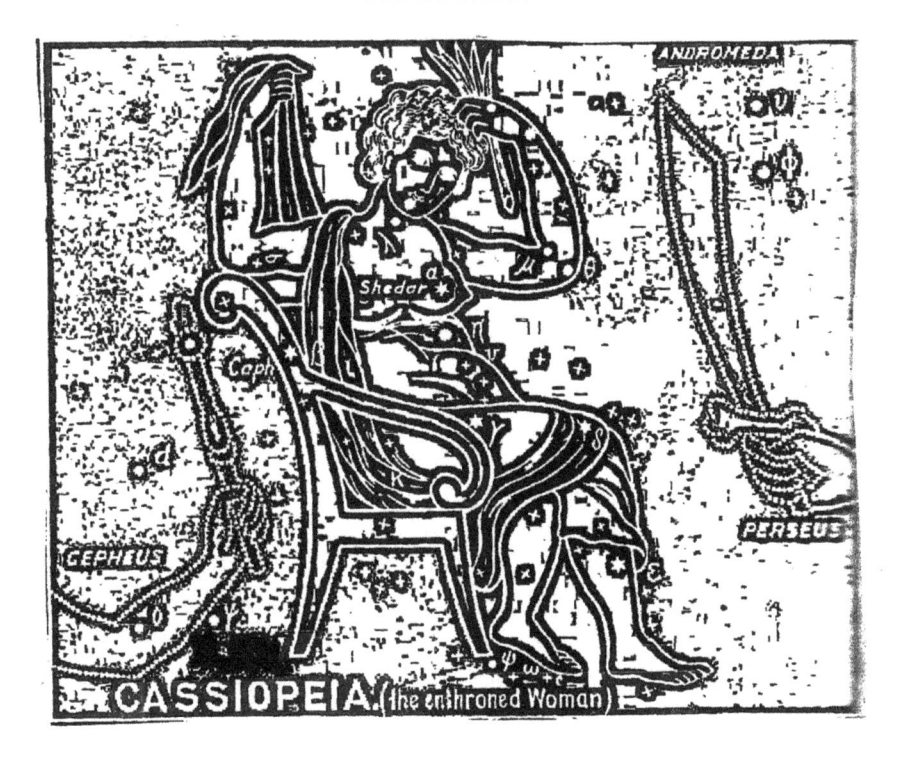

Cassiopeia
The Enthroned Woman
The Captive safe and delivered, and preparing for Her Husband, the Redeemer

This constellation is a picture of Jesus bride, "New Jerusalem." In this picture we see a woman in her hand the branch (Jesus). She is a Queen and has been Freed, from her captivity. This prophecy has not yet been fulfilled. It will be fulfilled after the seven years of Tribulation, and wedding fest of Christ.

It has 55 stars. The Hebrew word *Schedir,* means "Freed." The word Cassiopeia means "the beautiful and enthroned."

I have seen the modern-day Jerusalem, raped and bruised. It is missing three of its' original gates, and a big ugly ungodly mosque built on top of the Jewish Temple. Israel is partially free now and waiting for her redeemer.

Isaiah 45: 9 "Thy maker is thine husband, the Lord of Host is His name; the Holy One of Israel is your Redeemer, the God of the whole earth shall He be called. For the Lord has called thee woman forsaken and grieved in spirit. Even a wife of a youth when cast off, says thee God. For a small moment I have forsaken thee, but with great mercies will I gather thee, in overflowing wrath I hid my face from thee, saith the Lord thy Redeemer."

Psalm 45:9 "at the right hand does stand the Queen in Gold and Ophur."

This will be were all the Redeemed will live during the 1,000 years of Peace.

It will be beautiful beyond believe. A beautiful prophecy yet to come.

Praise the Lord Jesus, and pray for His emanate (immediate) return. Amen

Aries

The Bride of Christ
New Jerusalem

Set up as a queen, enthroned and beautiful.

The Freed, The Lamb's Wife, the Heavenly City of New Jerusalem

Cetus
(The Sea Monster)
The Great Enemy Bound

Cetus
The Sea Monster is Bound

This constellations' prophecy is that the great Dagon in the Sea will be bound and thrown into a bottomless pity. It is one of the largest constellations in area. It has 97 stars. The Hebrew word *Menke*, means "the bound." The Hebrew word *Mira*, means "the rebel." Satan surely is the rebel leader. This prophecy is yet to be fulfilled. This will happen after the Tribulation, just before the 1,000 years of Peace.

Job 4; 1 "can you draw leviathan with a hook?"

Isaiah 27 says this; "In the day of the Lord, with His sore and great strong sword, shall punish Leviathan, that piecing serpent, the crooked serpent, He shall slay the dragon that is in the sea."

Revelation 20: 1-3 "I saw an angel come down from heaven, having the key of the bottomless pit and a great chain in his hand. And he laid hold of that old serpent, which is the Devil, and Satan, and bound him up, and set a seal upon him, that he should deceive no more, till the thousand years should be fulfilled."

In the picture you can see the Band of Pisces is rapped around Cetus neck, choking him, while above his head Aries the Ram is stepping on him, crushing him. And Taurus the bull is rushing towards him. This is a prophecy of how Jesus and the Saints overwhelm the Devil after The Battle of Armageddon, subduing him and tossing him into the bottomless pit, bound and chained for 1,000 years. After which he will be freed for a short time.

Perseus
(The Breaker)
"The Breaker" Delivering His Redeemed

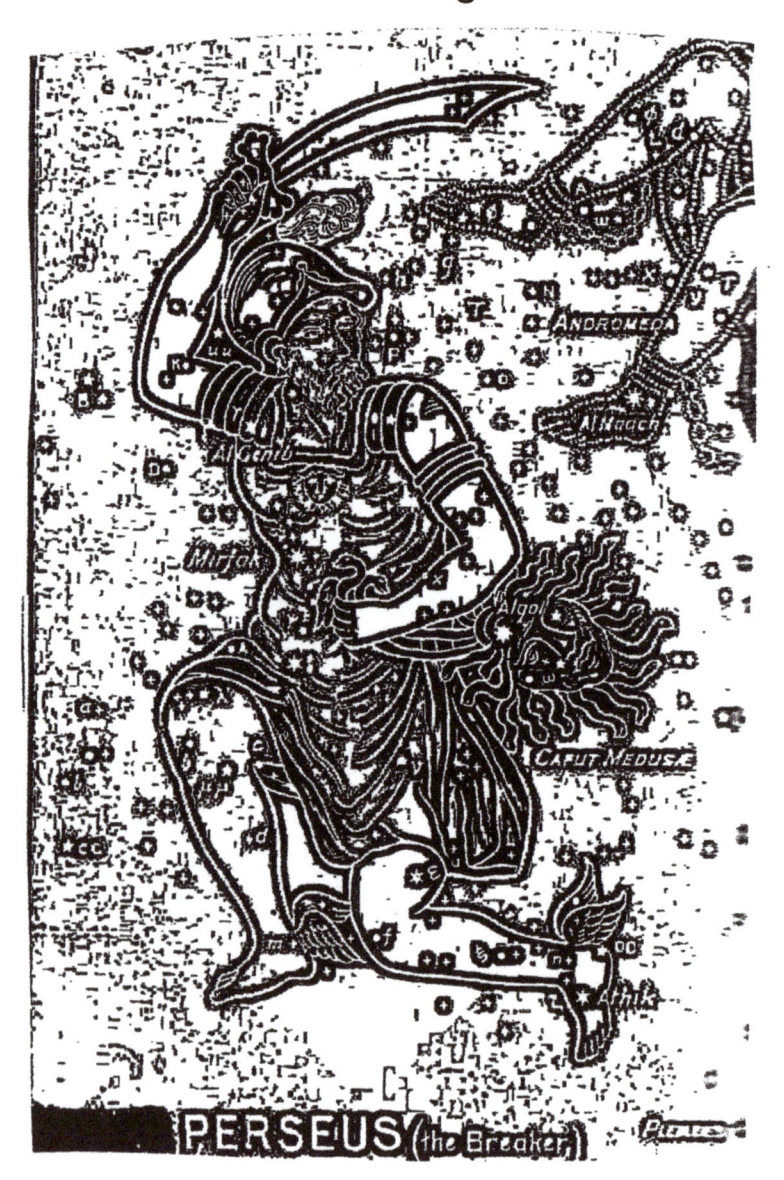

Perseus
The Breaker delivering His Redeemed

This constellation is a picture of what Jesus will do at the Battle of Armageddon. Its' prophecy is that Satan is defeated, freeing Cassiopeia (Jerusalem). This will happen during the Tribulation, when the Ruminate of Israel is redeemed.

In the picture you can see Perseus carrying the head of His enemy in His left hand, and a mighty sword, in His right hand. Breaking the Anti-Christ and His enemies, and doing it swiftly, with wings on His feet. This constellation has 59 stars. The Hebrew word *Rosh Satan*, means "the head of the adversary."

Micah 2:13 "The Breaker has come up before them, they have broken up, and have passed through the gate, and are gone out by it, and their king shall pass before them, and the Lord on the head of them."

Hebrews 9:28 "His coming to this earth, not for suffering for sin, but it will be a coming in Power, to Judge the earth, in Righteousness, and to subdue All Enemies, Under His feet.

This is when the Jewish tribes will be restored. Amen

CHAPTER SEVEN

Cancer
The Crab
The Messiah's possessions held fast

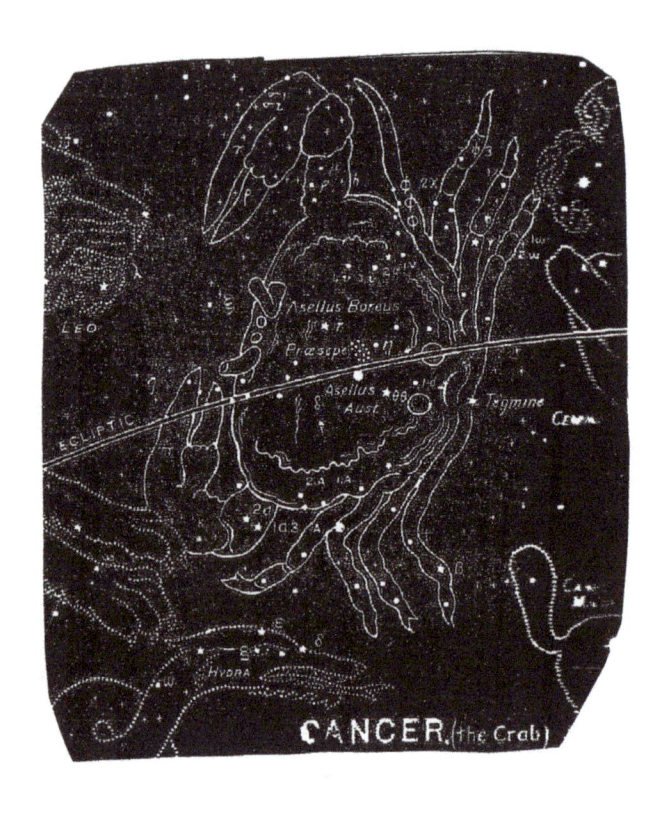

Chapter Seven
Cancer
The Crab
The Messiah's possessions held fast

This is a fascinating constellation, with a fascinating prophecy. This prophecy proves what I have always believed, that there are "holding places," both for heaven and for hell. Cancer is the "resting place,' for those who have died in Christ Jesus. A place of rest and peace, while waiting for the return of Jesus. The "Good News" is this has been happening, since Jesus returned to heaven.

We are under a different covenant with Jesus, than the Jews of the Old Testament were with God. When they died, they were sent to and held in "Hades." Hades was emptied out of all the Righteous Jews by Jesus when He rose from the dead. It is said, when He rose from Hades that it was seen by over 5,000 people who witnessed this in the streets of Jerusalem. Hades is located somewhere near or in Jerusalem, and is still a holding place for Hell.

He went to prepare a place for His Redeemed, a place of rest and peace for His "Saints," who have and will, die in His name, while waiting for His return.

This prophecy has been partially fulfilled. It will be fulfilled when Jesus returns.

Cancer is that holding place, far above the earth where the devil can not find it. It is in the "Milky Way." Cancer has 83 stars. It was assigned to the Tribe of Issachar described in Genesis 49: 14 "Issachar is a strong ass."

The number 69 turned sideways represents two asses, one pointing North and the other pointing South.

The Hebrew word *Asellus*, means "ass." Asellus Boras is the Northern Ass. And Asellus Australis is the Southern Ass.

The modern name for Cancer is the "Bee Hive." An ancient name for Cancer is "*Praesepe*," meaning "a multitude of the off spring.' This name fits the prophecy, as we are Gods children, His offspring, and we are being gathered together, getting ready for Jesus return. The dead in Christ will rise first. Amen

Ursa Minor
The Lesser Bear
The Gathering of the Jewish Ruminate

This constellations prophecy is for the Jewish Ruminate. It is represents' their "holding place" in Cancer a place of peace rest and peace. The Jewish people represent the smaller portion of the Redeemed under Jesus covenant. Jesus came for the "lost sheep of Israel," but they rejected Him. So, the gathering is smaller than the Gentile Sea. This prophecy is being fulfilled daily and will continue to be fulfilled. It has 24 stars. The Hebrew word *Dohu*, means "bear." The Hebrew word *Dohver*, means "a fold." This is the Jewish ruminates fold. This fold, is compared to the stars in heaven, the less fold. The big bear, is compared to the sands in the seas, the larger fold. This constellation is representative of Gods' holding place for Jews.

Usra Major
The Great Bear
The Gathering of the Fold and Flock of Jesus

This constellations prophecy is the gathering of all the Saints. This is the sea of the sands, those gentiles who have been grafted into the Jewish vine, under Jesus covenant with the Saints. It is being fulfilled and will continue to be fulfilled until His return. It has 87 stars. The Hebrew word *Dubhe*, means "a herd of animals." Another word *Merach*, means "the flock." *Phacada*, means "guarded or numbered."

Ezekiel 34: 12-16 "as a shepherd seeks out his flock, in the day that He is among His sheep that have scattered, so will I seek out My Sheep, and will deliver them out of places where they have been scattered in the cloudy and darkened day."

Jerimiah 31:10 "He that scattered Israel, will gather them."

Obadiah 2; 17 "but upon Mount Zion shall be deliverance."

This is Jesus holding place for His Saints. Because the harvest of the gentiles will be larger than the Jews.

Ursa Minor
The Lesser Bear

Ursa Major

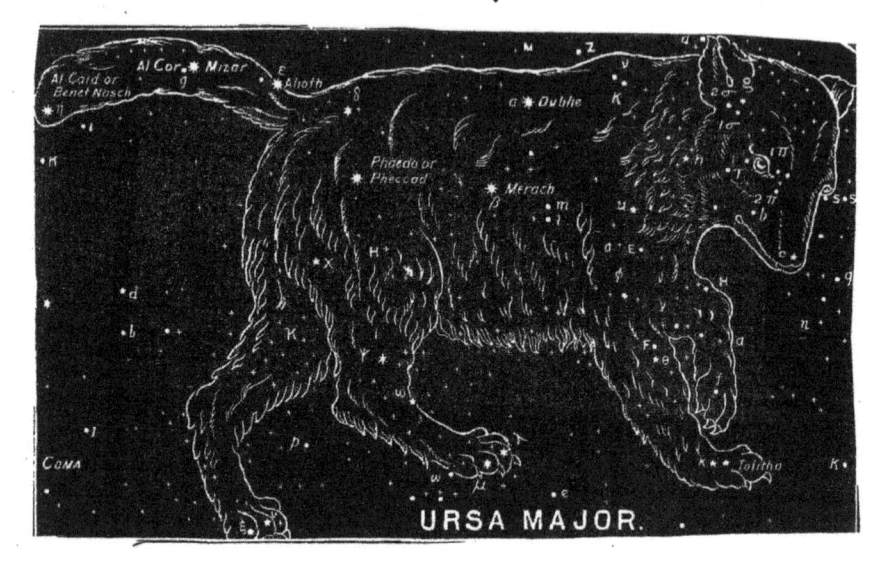

The Gathering

Chapter Seven continued
Argo
The Old Ship of Zion

Agro
The Old Ship of Zion

This prophecy is that a great ship is waiting in port to take all the Redeemed to Zion (heaven). Our travel arrangements have already been made. It is for those who died in Christ. They will be taken to heaven by this ship. It is yet to be fulfilled. It will happen at the "catching up." Noah's Ark was a type of this happening in the Old Testament. Argo has 64 stars.

Isaiah 60:9 "the ships of "Tarshish" to bring our sons from afar."

Isaiah 35: 9 "and the ransom of the Lord shall return and come to Zion with songs."

Aratus sang this of Argo; "Stern-foremost hauled, no mark of onward speeding ship. Sternward she comes, as vessels do, when sailors turn the helm. On entering harbor, all oars back in the water, and guiding backwards to the anchor comes.'

In the picture Argo is a mighty ship, with many oars, backing in port. With a huge sail and the head of a Lion on its bow. The word *Canopus* or *Camobus*, means "in possession of Him who comes."

What a blessing this prophecy has been and continue to be. Praise the Lord Jesus Christ. Amen

CHAPTER EIGHT

Pisces

The Fish and the Band

Chapter Eight
Pisces
The Fish and the Band
An abundance of Blessing for the Redeemed

This is a prophecy of the Saints and the Ruminate of Jewish people being Redeemed. This constellation has 23 stars. It was assigned to the tribe of Simeon. It is a picture of two fish bound together by a band. One fish is pointing heavenly and the other is neither up or down. This is the great prophecy of how the redeemed will be rescued. Those Saints in Christ, are with the fish pointing up. The Jewish ruminate, is the fish just swimming along the equator. They will be "caught up alive," during the Tribulation.

The Hebrew word *Dagum*, means "the fishes."

Ezekiel 47:9 "there shall be a great multitude of fish."

Constellations that support Pisces prophecy are; The Band, Andromeda and Cepheus.

The Band

The band was a mystery constellation, it's meaning was kept a secret, that wasn't revealed until the arrival of Jesus.

Romans 16:25 "It was kept as secret since the world began."

Ephesians 3:9 "from the beginning of the world hath been hid in God."

Colossians 1:26 "hath been hid from ages and from generations, but now made manifest to His saints."

Hosea 11: 4 "I drew them with cords, and bands of love."

The mystery was revealed by Paul in 1 Thessalonians 4: 16-18

"For the Lord Himself shall descend from Heaven with a shout, with the voice of the Archangel, and with a trump of God: and the dead in Christ shall rise first, then we which are alive and remain shall be caught up together with them in the clouds, to meet the Lord in the air, and so shall we ever be with the Lord. Take comfort in these words."

I had this dream as a child, and wrote about it in my first book.

The Jews of old, did not have a redeemer. They had to be Righteous in order to get to heaven.

The Jews of today need a redeemer, they need to find Jesus. The first question Jesus will ask you is this; "What have you done for my people?" Amen

Andromeda
(the chained Woman)

Andromeda
The Chained Woman

This is an interesting prophecy. The constellation of Andromeda represents the Holy City of God here on earth, "Jerusalem." The picture is of a Queen, bound in chains, both ankles and hands. You can see the down fish of Pisces coming for her. This prophecy is still being fulfilled. Jerusalem is a beaten down city, three of it's gates are missing. The Muslims have built a temple on top of the Jewish temple there. She will continue be bound until Jesus returns from His wedding fest, after the 7 years of Tribulation and God's wrath, we the Redeemed, will live in "New Jerusalem," during Jesus 1,000 years reign of Peace.

There are 63 stars in Andromeda. The Hebrew word *Sirra*, means "the chained."

Jerimiah 14:7 "for the virgin daughter of my people is broken with a great breach, with a grievous blow."

Yes, Jerusalem and Israel were wiped off the face of the earth for 2,000 years. The Jews scattered to many nations.

Isaiah 51:3 "for the Lord shall comport Zion, He will comfort all her wastes places; and he will make her wilderness like Eden, and her desert like the garden of the Lord."

This prophecy has been fulfilled on May 15, 1948, when Israel became a nation again. But the prophecy of "New Jerusalem," is yet to be completed.

She is freed but still need a redeemer.

Cepheus
The Redeemer comes to Rule

This constellation completes the prophecy of, Jesus coming back and being Crowned as the King of Kings and Lord of Lords, He rescues Israel and brings Jerusalem back, restored to being beautiful and loved. Reborn as "New Jerusalem," a city of peace and love. Its' pillars will bear the names of all the Redeemed. In the picture you see a crown of stars on Cepheus head. In His left hand is a scepter. In His right hand, a blanket to warm and comfort Andromeda. This constellation has 35 stars.

The Hebrew word *Cepheus*, means "the Branch." Jesus is the Branch of Israel.

Exodus 4:22 "thus says the Lord, Israel is my son, even my first born.'

This prophecy will happen after the Tribulation.

CHAPTER NINE

Gemini
The Twins

Chapter Nine
Gemini
The Twins

This constellation has a prophecy that is both complexed and comprehensive.

Its' prophecy is that once the Holy Spirit is with you, it never leaves you, and you will have two natures, carnal man and Godly spiritual. Gemini was assigned to the Tribe of Benjamin. It has 85 stars.

The picture shows us two people, coming together

It is God and Jesus. Gemini prophesies that Jesus is coming to Reign in the 1,000 years of peace. He is coming with God the Father. They will throw Satan into a bottomless pit. They come in brotherhood, united in fellowship. The Hebrew word *Thaumum* means "united." These twins are heavy armed, with bow and arrows, and a large club. One is carrying a harp to celebrate a great victory. The Hebrew word *Twinned* means "doubled." It is double trouble for Satan and his angels, and the unbelievers. God is coming back with Jesus this time.

Woo unto the ungodly when these twins come back in wrath.

Gemini represents "Salvation" for Jesus and for His redeemed. Amen

Psalm 37:38 "as for transgressors, they shall be destroyed together."

Psalm 72: 7 "in His days the righteous shall flourish, and there will be an abundance of peace so long as the moons endures.'

Isaiah 45:2 "look unto me, and you shall be saved, over all the ends of the earth.

Another mystery has been solved; God is coming back with His Son.

When your ship is in a storm, look to the Masters nail scared hands. You have been washed in the blood of the Lamb. He is your lighthouse on the stormy sea, and lonely nights. Praise the Lords name. Amen

Gemini has three supporting constellations they are; Lupus, Canis Major and Canis Minor.

Chapter Nine
Lepus
The Hare or Enemy

Lepus
The Hare
The Enemy being trodden underfoot

This constellation is the prophecy that Satan will be crushed by the conquering Lion of Judah (Jesus). It has 19 stars. The Hebrew word *Arnebo*, means "the enemy of Him who comes." If you look at the picture you see the hare is under the foot of Orion. Lepus is about to be crushed.

Isaiah 63:3-4

"I will tread them in my anger, and trample them in my fury, for the day of vengeance is in my heart, and the year of my redeemed is to come."

This prophecy is yet to come true. We know the enemy is still here, lying, deceiving and stealing.

Canis Major
The Big Dog
Sirius the Prince

This constellation is a type of God, the Big Dog. Its' prophecy is this; He comes with His companion Jesus (the lesser dog) in brotherhood, to destroy their enemies. It has 64 stars The Hebrew word *Abur*, means "the mighty," the Big Dog is God Almighty.

This constellation is seen in the summer, hence our saying: "the dog days of summer."

Homer said this of Sirius: "whose burning taints the red air with fevers, plagues, and death."

This speaks to the book of Revelation and Gods wrath of plagues and scorpions, He will send in the "last days."

This will happen during the Tribulation.

Prophecy Written in the Stars

Canis Minor
The Lesser Dog
The Exalted Redeemer

This constellation is the prophecy of Jesus, the Son of God, and Gods companion in brotherhood. He is coming with His father to destroy their enemies. This will happen at the Tribulation. When they chain Satan and his angels and throw them into the bottomless pit. This constellation has 14 stars.

Isaiah 49:26 "All flesh shall know that I am the Lord and Savior, and redeemer, the mighty one of Jacob."

Isaiah 59:19 "and the redeemer shall come to Zion."

CHAPTER TEN

Sagittarius
The Archer

Chapter Ten
Sagittarius
The Archer

This constellation is a continuing of the prophecies against Satan. This constellation was assigned to the Tribe of Asher. It has 69 stars. The Hebrew name *Kesith*, means "the archer." Other Hebrew names of stars are *Knem*, meaning "He conquers," and *Naim*, meaning "the gracious one." In the picture you see a creature that is half man and half horse. Having two natures, a powerful man armed with a ready bow and arrow, and with the ability of a mighty stallion, able to move swiftly. His arrow is pointed a Scorpio's heart.

This constellation is a type of the father God, coming in His wrath.

He will destroy the devil at" The Great White Throne Judgment." This prophecy is yet to be fulfilled.

Revelation 6:2 "He went forth to conquer."

Psalm 64:7-10 "God shall shoot at them with an arrow." Suddenly they shall be wounded."

John in Revelation says; "I saw a white horse and Him that sat on it, He had a bow, and He went forth conquering."

Aratus sang this about Sagittarius; "Midst golden stars, He stands refulgent now, and thrust the scorpion with His bow."

The arrow of God kills His enemies. There are three constellations that support this prophecy, they are; Lyra, Ara, and Draco.

Lyra
The Harp
Praise being prepared for the Conqueror

This is a nice prophecy that there will be Rejoicing and Celebration in Zion, When Jesus is finally Crowned King of Kings. Lyra has a star in it named *Vega*, which means "He shall be exalted." Another star name is *Gnasor*, meaning "a Harp."

Psalm 21:13 "be thou exalted, Lord in thine own strength, so will we sing and praise thy power."

Psalm 65:1 "Praise waits for thee, O God of Zion."

Exodus 15:1 "then sang Moses and the children of Israel this song unto the Lord."

Amen Praise Jesus Lord of Lords, the Alpha and the Omega.

Ara

The Consuming Fire being prepared for His Enemies

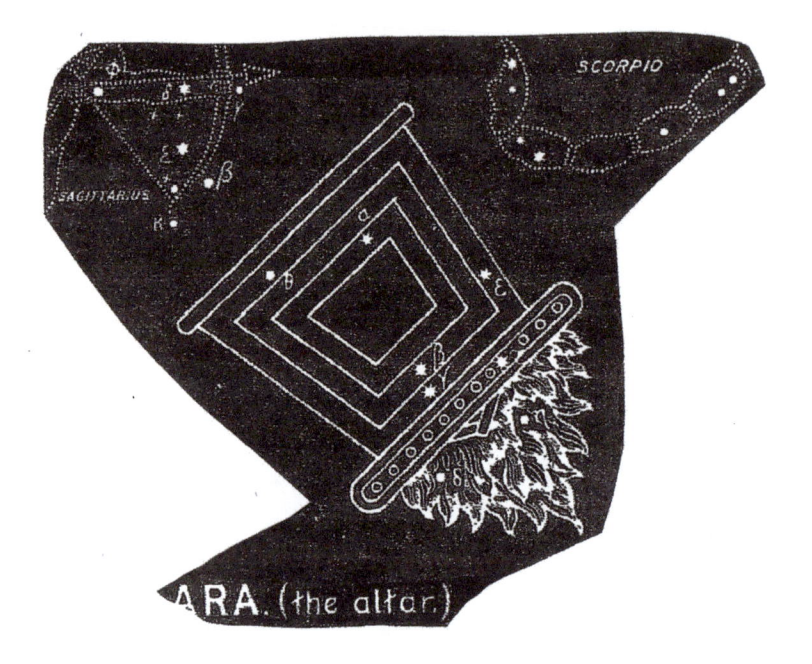

This constellations prophecy is of the coming "Lake of Fire" for Satan and his angels. It is a small constellation with 9 stars. This prophecy is of the Great White Throne Judgment, yet to be fulfilled. It is said that all the saints will be there to witness this event.

Psalm 21:9 "thou shalt make them as a fiery oven in the time of thine anger, the Lord shall swallow them up in His wrath, and the fire shall devour them.'

Isaiah 63:4 "for the day of vengeance is in His heart."

This is the fire that consumes all the unbelievers.

Draco
The Dragon that old serpent
Cast down from heaven

This constellation is further proof that Sagittarius represents God and His prophecy. God is who cast Satan from heaven. Draco is a long slithering 80 stars of snake. Part of this prophecy has been fulfilled. Satan has been thrown to earth. His next throw will be into the Bottomess pit, and then the Lake of fire, represented by Ara. Satan that great seducer, father of lies, and thief, will burning forever and ever in Hell. The Hebrew word *Dahrach* means "to tread on." In the picture the hoofs of Sagittarius are treading on the head of the snake. Anther Hebrew word *Rastaban* means "the head of the serpent."

Isaiah 27:1 "and He shall slay the dragon that is in the sea."

Revelation 12:9-10 "the great dragon was cast out, that old serpent, called the devil and Satan, which deceives the whole world, he was cast out and his angels with him, and I heard a voice saying in Heaven, now is come salvation, and strength, and the Kingdom of God, and the power of His Christ; for the accuser of our brethren is cast down." Amen

Draco
The Dragon that old serpent
Cast down from heaven

CHAPTER ELEVEN

Taurus

The Bull

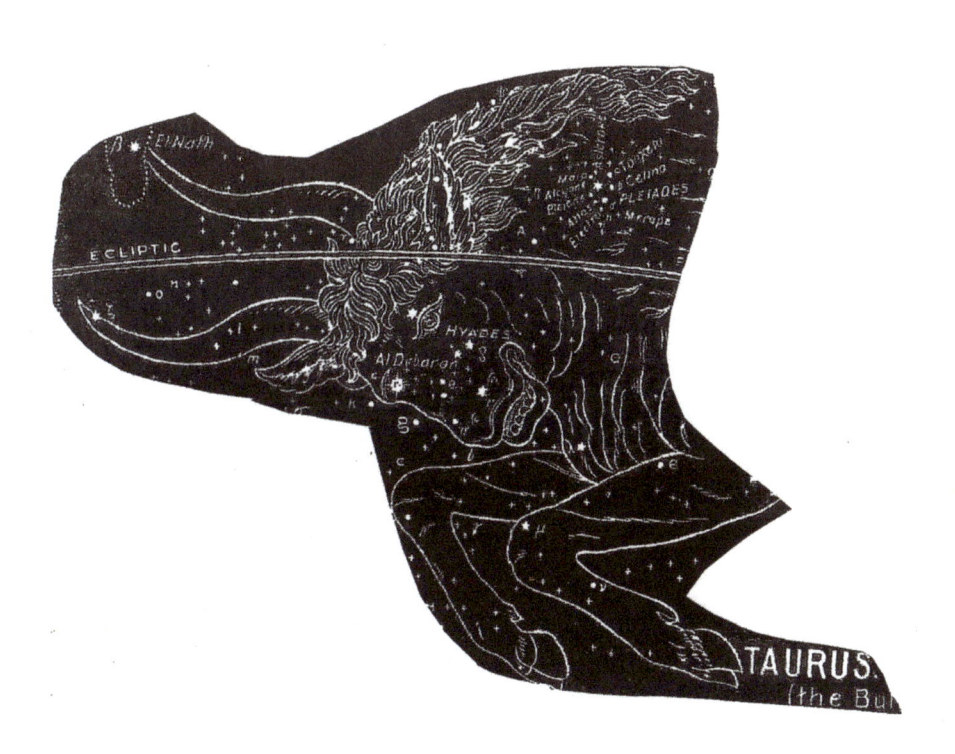

Chapter Eleven
Taurus
The Bull

This is a nice and interesting prophecy in the constellation of the Bull, it is a message for all the Saints. Its' prophecy is the Jesus as a Large Horned charging Bull, will lead His Army of Saints. The Bull is charging the enemy. This will happen at "The Battle of Armageddon." This is after the Tribulation. The Bull was assigned to the Tribes of Ephrain and Manasseth, by their brother Joseph, who assigned all the Tribes. The horns of the Bull represent the two tribes, this is a powerful beast. There are 141 stars in it. This constellation contains the "*Pleiades*," Who's meaning is "the congregation of the Judge, or Ruler." This would apply to the Saints accompanying Jesus to the battle. The Hebrew word *Chim* means "accumulation."

Another group of stars in the Bull are the "Hyades." Meaning "the congregation."

And the Hebrew word *Palilicium* means "belonging to the judge."

Jesus is coming to judge the world, and He is bringing His Saints with Him. Jude 14-15

"and Enoch, also the seventh from Adam, prophesied of these sayings, Behold the Lord comes with ten thousands of His Saints." Amen it is prophesized by Enoch.

Deuteronomy 33:7

"the first of His bullock majesty is His, and His Horns of the Wild Ox.'

This is a prophecy of the coming Judge and Judgment.

Isaiah 13:11-15

"I will punish the world for their evil, and the wicked for their iniquity."

Isaiah 34:2

"for the Lord has indignation against All Nations."

Jesus is coming soon.

Orion
The Lion from the Tribe of Judah
The coming King of Kings, Prince of Peace

This constellation is a continuance of the glory of the Risen Christ. The prophecy here is that Jesus comes back and He saves the Tribes of Israel. They see the light and are no longer blind. This will happen during the Tribulation. There are 78 stars in Orion. In the picture we see a mighty man with a large club in one hand and the head of a lion in the other hand. He is stepping on Lepus the hare, crushing it.

Job speaks of Orion in his book.

Isaiah 42:13 "the Lord shall go forth as a mighty man."

Isaiah 60:1 "and the gentiles shall come to the light, and kings to the brightness of thy rising."

A Hebrew word *Betelgeuz* means "the branch" Jesus is the Branch.

The star *Bellatrix* means "the branch comes."

Another Hebrew word is *Oarion* meaning "bring the light forth from Heaven."

Like the song; "This little light of mine." Orion lights up the night sky. A constant reminder that Jesus is Victorious and coming soon.

Aratus sang this song; "Eastward beyond the region of the Bull, stands Great Orion, and who, when the night is clear, beholds Him gleaming bright, shall cast his eyes in vain, to find a sign more Glorious in all of Heaven." Amen

Wow preacher have even preached on the subject of the Gentiles coming to the light?

Orion
The Lion from the Tribe of Judah
The coming King of Kings, Prince of Peace

Eridanus
The River of Gods' Wrath and Judgment

This constellations prophecy is that a "river of tears" will be cried by the unbelievers as they are thrown into the Lake of Fire at the Great White Throne Judgment. It will be molten hot tears of those thrown in the Lake of Fire. There are 84 stars in Eridanus. The ancient Hebrew word *Archerar* means "the after part of a river."

The prophecy Daniel sees a river in a vision. "I beheld a fiery stream issued and came forth from Him."

Psalm 97:3-5 "A fire goes before Him, the light of the whole earth."

Habakkuk 12:5 "His brightness was as the light.'

Aratus sang this; "For yonder trod by heavenly feet, wind the scorched waters of Eridanus tear-swollen flood, welling beneath Orion's foot."

Look Up
And be watchful
For the end is near
Prophecies have been foretold
And we can clearly read the signs
The stars and the gospels tell us
This is not our home
Jesus is coming again
We know not the hour or the day
With a Hallelujah cry, He will split the Eastern Sky
He is on His way
So, look up and be watchful
And don't be left behind

Eridanus
The River of Judgment
The Wrath of God poured out on His enemies

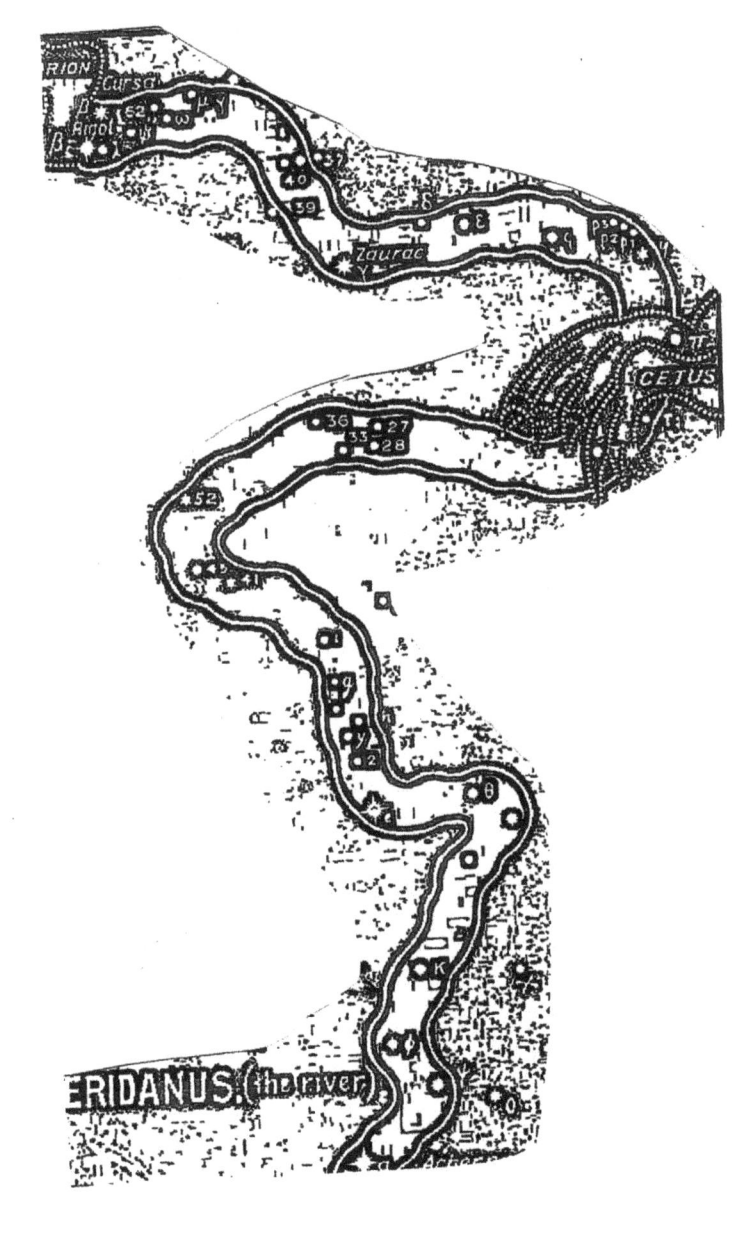

Auriga
The Shepherd comes and there is Safety for the Redeemed

This constellation is a prophecy of Jesus protection of the Redeemed from the wrath that is coming from God (The rushing Bull). It has 66 stars. The word *Auriga* is a Hebrew root word meaning "shepherd." In the picture you see a she goat on the shepherds left arm. The Hebrew word *Alioth* means "a she goat." The Hebrew word *Menkilinon* has the meaning "chain of goats.' Another Hebrew word *Maaz* means "a flock of goats." It's prophecy proves the Apostle Paul right when he prophesies in 1 Thessalonians and 1 Corinthians, that the Saints, the true Believers, will not suffer the Tribulation, and those living, will be caught up alive…Amen.. A mystery is solved. Amen

Ezekiel 34:22 "I will save my flock, and they shall no longer be prey and have one shepherd."

Jeremiah 23:4 "and they shall fear no more, nor be dismayed, neither shall they be lacking. Saith the Lord."

1 Peter 4:17 "for the time has come that judgment must begin at the House of God."

Isaiah 45:22 "look unto me, and be saved, O all ye ends of the earth."

Isaiah 40:11 "He shall feed His flock like a shepherd; he shall gather the lambs with His arm."

Aratus sang this; "She is both large and bright, but they the kids, shine somewhat feebly on Auriga's wrist."

Hebrews 13:20 "Lord Jesus, that Great shepherd."

Isaiah 40:10-11 "Behold the Lord God as a mighty one, and His arm shall rule for Him,; Behold His reward is with Him, and His recompense before Him; He shall feed His flock like a shepherd, He shall gather His lambs in His arms and carry them in His bosom, and shall gently lead those that give suck.'

The Lord is our Tower of Refuse. Amen

Auriga
The Shepherd comes and there is Safety for the Redeemed

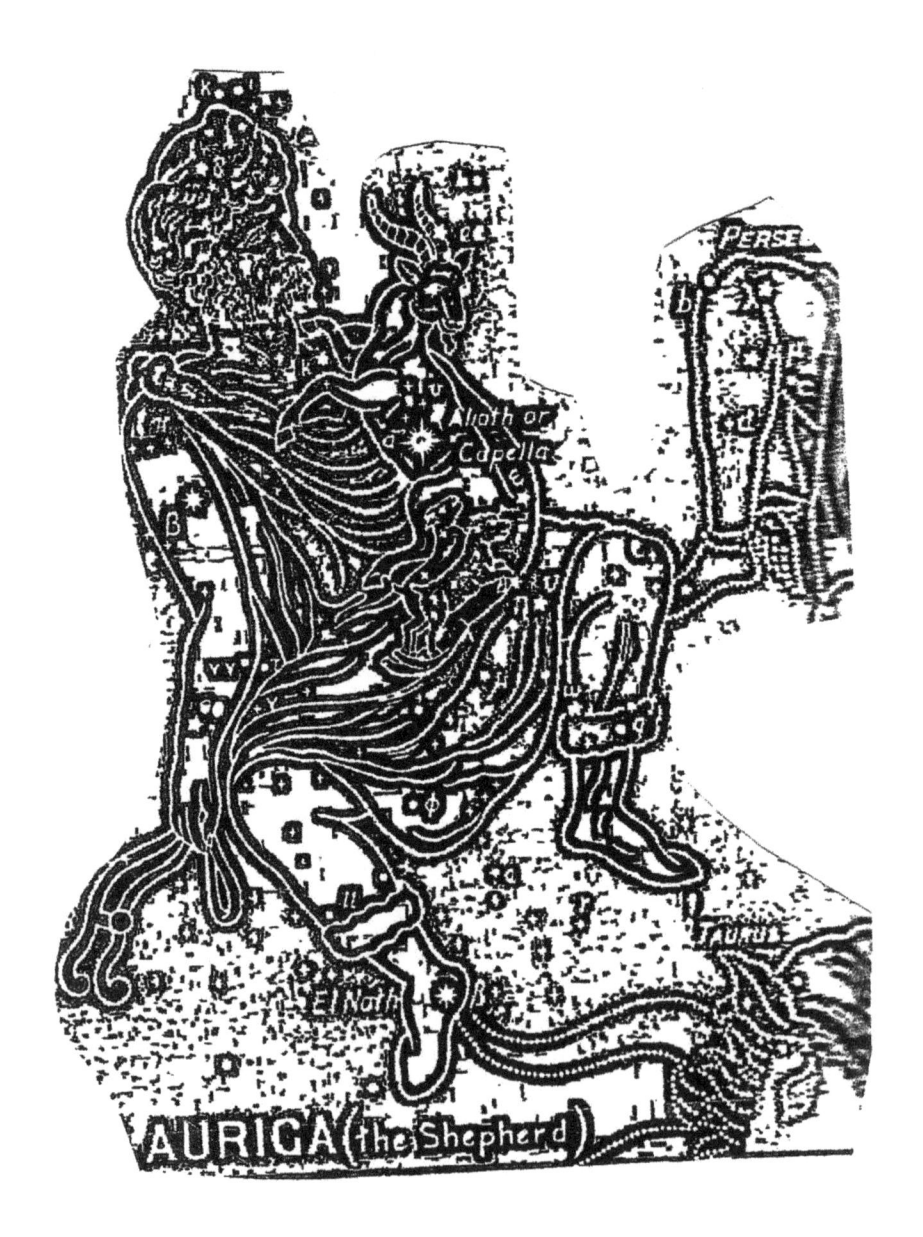

CHAPTER TWELVE

Leo

The Lion

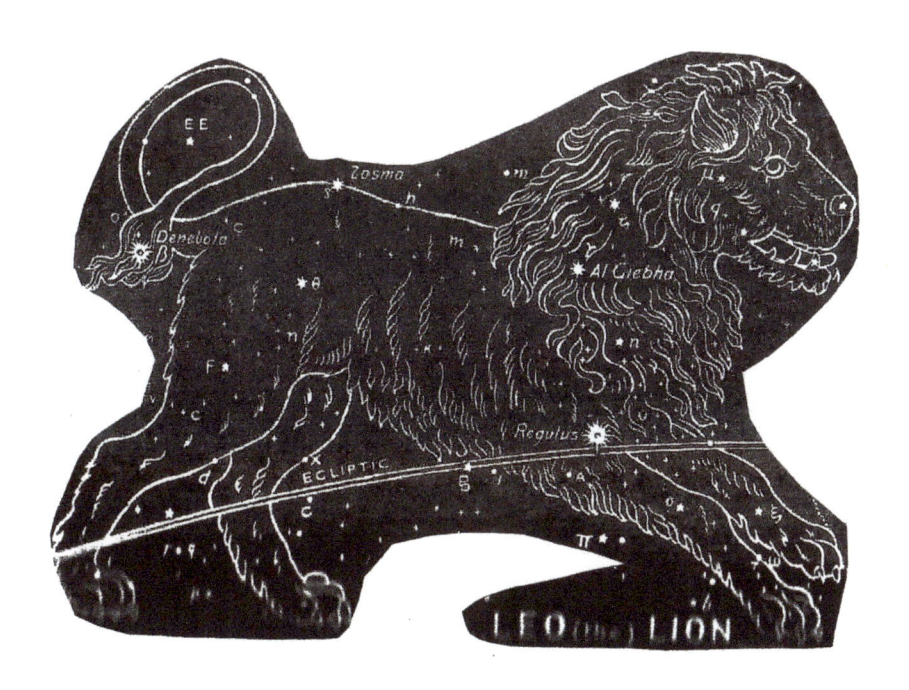

Chapter Twelve
Leo
The Lion

This is the most important constellation of the Forty-Eight we are studying. Its' prophecy is the most important. It means all pain and sorrow and strife are over; Amen. This is the prophecy that all the Saints have been waiting for. The return of Christ, He comes back as the "Conquering Lion from the Tribe of Judah." The picture is of a huge male lion. It is trampling on the serpent hydra, and is on the prowl for its' prey. This is a picture of Jesus when He returns, hunting down the enemies of God. The Lion from the Tribe of Judah has been aroused. Leo was assigned to the Tribe of Judah, and has 95 stars. It has three supporting constellations, Hydra, Crater, and Corvus

Here are four stars with Hebrew names and meanings.

Arieh "the lion, hunting prey."

Minchir "tearing of the lion."

Regulus "treading under foot."

Denebola "the judge who comes."

Genesis 49:9 "Thy hand shall be on the neck of thine enemies; Judah is a lions' whelp."

Amos asked "will a lion roar in the forest, when He has no prey."

Jesus certainly has prey and He will be roaring.

Nahum 2:12 "the lion did tear in pieces enough for His whelps."

2 Samuel 17:10 "and He also is valiant, whose heart is as the heart of a lion."

Numbers 24:9 "He shall eat up the nations, His enemies, and shall break their bones, and pierce them with His arrows, He is crouched, He lay down like a lion, and as a Great Lion. Who shall stir Him up?"

Revelation 5:5 "and one of the elders said unto me, weep not; behold the Lion from the Tribe of Judah." Amen and Amen

Hydra
That old serpent destroyed

Crater
The Cup of Divine Wrath poured out on Satan

Corvus
The Raven, Bird of Prey, devouring the serpent

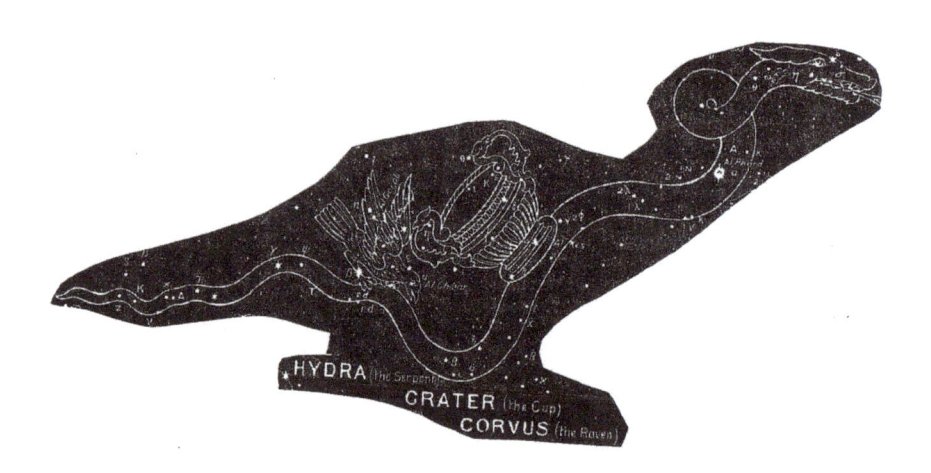

Hydra
That old serpent destroyed

This constellation is a picture of that old dragon and serpent Satan being destroyed, twisting in pain, and being eaten alive by birds of prey and God is pouring out His Devine Cup of wrath, scorching the snake. Hydra has 60 stars.

The word Hydra means "he is abhorred, loathed and hated."

Crater
The Cup of Divine Wrath, being poured out on the snake, Satan, the thief, the seducer, and father of all lies

This constellation has 13 stars. It's the prophecy that God will punish Satan. It also is the Cup of Wrath that will be poured out on the earth at the start of the Great seven years of Tribulation. *Al Ches* means "the cup."

Psalm 11:6 "upon the wicked He shall rain snares; fire and brimstone, and a horrible tempest; this shall be the portion of their cup."

Psalm 11:8

"and the wine red; it is full of mixture, and He pours out of the same; but the dregs therefore all the wicked of the earth shall wring them out and drink them."

Revelation 14:10 "the cup of wine of the fierceness of His wrath."

Corvus
The Raven, a bird of Prey, devouring the Serpent

This is an interesting prophecy Corvus gives us. It only has nine stars. The picture is of a Raven eating the serpent. This prophecy is what will happen after The Battle of Armageddon. The bible says that the blood of the dead will be as high as a horses' bridle, and the birds of prey will eat the flesh of the dead.

Proverbs 30:17 "the eye that mocks at his father, and despised, to obey his mother, the Ravens of the Valley will pick it out."

1 Samuel 17:46 "I will smite thee and take your head from thee and I will give the carcasses of the Host of the Philistines this day unto the fowls of the air, and the wild beast of the earth."

Revelation 19:17-18 "to all the fowls of the air that fly in the midst of Heaven come gather yourselves together unto the supper of the Great God."

It's not too late

No matter what you have done His mercy can show you grace.

But I wouldn't hesitate

I wouldn't want to face Him on the Judgment Day

Without His mercy and grace

So, look up and be watchful and

Don't be Left Behind

Look up to the Master

CHAPTER THIRTEEN

Libra

(The Scales)

This constellation was assigned to the Tribe of Levi.

This constellation has 51 stars in it.

It prophesizes the *Redeemers Atoning Work*. Jesus paid the price to balance the scales. He purchased the price for redemption.

Libra
The Scales
Judgment on the Cross, The Victim, The Crown

Chapter Thirteen
Libra
*The Scales, the Redeemers Atoning Work,
the Price Paid by Jesus*

This constellations prophecy is the Atoning work of Christ. It is a picture of the "Holy Altar," where Judgment was made on the Cross. Jesus paid the price for mankind's' sin debt. He paid the Ransom to set us free. The scales have been balanced. This prophecy has been fulfilled, Praise the Lord Jesus, our Redeemer and savior. Amen

It's not too late to say you are sorry

It's not to late to say you want to change

Is that too much to ask you for

When He offers you, His mercy and His Grace?

I wouldn't want to face Him without it on the Judgment Day

The Hebrew word *Mozanaim means* "the scales." Zeben al Genubi means "the purchase."

Isaiah 40:7 "Who has measured the waters in the hollow of His hand, and meted out Heaven with the span, and comprehended the dust of the Earth in a measure, and weighted the mountains in a Scale, and the hills in a Balance?"

Who? The answer is Lord Jesus Christ, that's who Amen!

Psalm 49:7 "none of them can by any means redeem his brother, nor give to God a ransom for him. For the redemption of their soul is costly, and must be done forever."

Jesus is the only one who can redeem us.

Revelation 5:9 a new song is sung "Thou art worthy for thou were slain and has rose from the grave and redeemed us to God by your blood."

Have you been washed by the blood of Jesus?

John 5:24 "We pass from death to Life."

Libra has three supporting constellations, The Crux, Lupus, and Corona.

Libra
The Scales
Judgment on the Cross, The Victim, The Crown

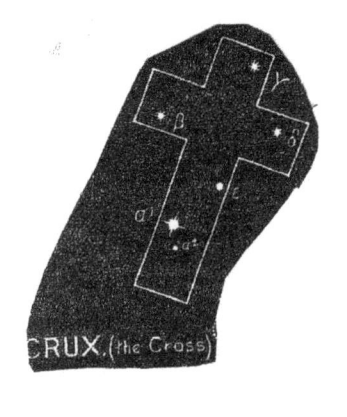

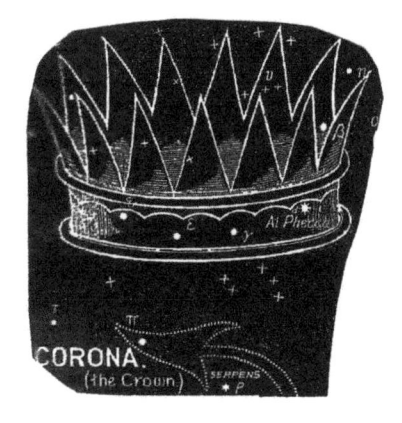

Crux
The Cross

This is the smallest constellation with only 4 stars. Crux's prophecy is of Jesus being crucified on the cross. And, of course it has already been fulfilled. I have been to Golgotha "the skull," as described in John 19:17. It is a small hill, that looks like the face Jesus staring back at you, you can see His beard, vary eerie. The Garden Tomb is right next to Golgotha, just like the bible says. The stone is gone but the groove it was in is still there. The Hebrew word *Tau* means "a mark." And *Adam* means "to be cut off.' The ancient Christians used to mark their coins with an x, for the cross.

Dante sang a song: "the four stars never beheld; but by the early race of men."

Daniel 9:26 "after threescore and two weeks shall Messiah be cut off."

Ephesians 2:12-13 "ye who sometimes were far off, are now made nigh by the Blood of Christ."

John 5:24 "passed from death to Life,"

The door has been opened for the Gentiles. Jesus has Blessed us; we have been washed in His blood. Grafted into the vine of the Chosen.

Lupus
The Victim Slain

This is the fulfillment of the prophecy of the Crux. Jesus is the Victim. He was falsely charged and crucified on the cross. This prophecy has been fulfilled. This constellation has 22 stars.

The Hebrew word *Asedad* means "to be slain."

John 19:17 "And they took Jesus, and lead Him away. And He bearing His cross, went forth into a place called "the place of the skull," which in Hebrew is called Golgotha."

John 10:15 "He offered Himself without spot to God."

Hebrews 9: 26 "He put way sin, by scarifying Himself.'

Philippines 2:5 "He humbled Himself, and became obedient unto death, even the death on the cross.'

shearers is dumb, so He opened not His mouth."

In the picture we see Lupus the victim falling down dead.

Death on the cross-means Life for the repentant sinner. Amen

Corona
The Crown Bestowed

This constellation is the reason I selected Libra as the last zodiac constellation to look at. Corona is the last of Gods prophecies written in the stars. This will be the fulfillment of Jesus being crown the King of Kings and Lord of Lords. This is the crown that will bestowed on our Christ, our Redeemer, and the Son of God. Amen Corona has 21 stars. *Ataroth* is a Hebrew name meaning; "A Royal Crown." This is the end of the prophecies written in the stars, Jesus receiving His crown.

Hebrews 2:9 "for suffering the death, for every man, crowned with Glory and Honor."

Revelation 5;9 "thou was slain and have redeemed us to God the Father."

CHAPTER FOURTEEN

Predestination or Did it Hurt when You Fell from Heaven?

John 3:13 "and no man has ascended to Heaven but he that came down from Heaven."

This pretty much sums up where our Spirits came from. They were sent from heaven by God, to this earth to find our way back to Heaven.

The great debate of our times; Who is predestine to heaven? Well Jesus says we all are predestine, the question is to where? Jesus said Judas Iscariot was predestine to Hell (John 6:70). So, predestination is a two-way street. So, the question then is, where are you predestine to, Heaven or Hell? Did you volunteer to come here? Or were you sent here?

Romans 8:29 "For He already knew, He was predestined to conform to the image of His Son."

Ephesians 1:5 "having predestined us to be adopted by His Son Jesus the Christ."

John 14:6 "I am the truth and the life. No man comes before the Father but by me."

Luke 11:23 "he who is not with me, is against me."

Those against Jesus, need us that are for Him, to shine our own "Little Light" on them. Amen

The bible says that this earth is clearly not our home. The prophecy of the stars tells us this is not our home.

Romans 1 says that we are all called to be Saints. But some of us chose not to believe.

And Romans 8:29 says that Gods goal is for all of us to be Saints, but He gave man freedom of choice, and some chose to not believe.

Ephesians 1:11 says; "we are predestined according to Gods will. Which makes me think, He sent most of us here for a reason or two.

What is your destination, is it Heaven or Hell? It's in your hands.

Conclusion and Acknowledgments

My inspiration for writing this book, came from my studies on this subject while in seminary. I was studying a book written over 125 years ago. The subject was Prophecies written in the stars. The Reverend E. W. Bullinger D.D. wrote a book titled "Witness to the Stars." I own a gratitude of thanks to him for his comprehensive study of the stars' names. And to his illustrator MS Amy Manson whos' illustrations I have borrowed. I also borrowed illustrations from Arthur Waites' Tarot Card deck, drawn by Pamela Coleman Smith. I used the King James revision of the Bible. And MS Lise Lunser helped me to edit the book. The Holy Spirit inspired me to write a book that is meaningful to our times. May this book be a Blessing to you.

Dr. Larry Anderson, Glory Day & In The Spirit of Elijah Ministries.